The Sweet Potato Vines Story

By Maltee McMahon

"Love Grows: The Sweet Potato Vines Story," by Maltee McMahon. ISBN 978-1-63868-079-6 (softcover); 978-1-63868-080-2 (eBook).

Published 2022 by Virtualbookworm.com Publishing, P.O.Box 9949, College Station, TX, 77842, US.

©2022 Maltee McMahon. All rights reserved. No part of this publication may be reproduced, stored in a retrieval system, or transmitted in any form or by any means, electronic, mechanical, recording or otherwise, without the prior written permission of Maltee McMahon.

Once upon a time, I planted four sweet potato vine plants in a blue pot.

I loved this pot and the color of it.

I filled it up with soil and got ready to plant. I was so excited to plant these sweet potato plants. My favorite plants.

I loved the color of the leaves. I couldn't wait to watch them grow.

It was a great day for planting.

Every day, I waited patiently for the sweet potato vines to grow.

I took great care of my plants with water and said positive words.

I enjoyed talking with my plants every day.

I believed if I told them to grow, they would grow.

I told them how much I loved them. I told them to grow healthy and amazing.

And they grew ... and grew ... and grew. They seemed to grow really fast, like I asked them to. I continued to talk with them every day in a positive way with loving words.

Before long, the blue flower pot was covered with vines like a blanket. The vines looked healthy and happy.

I thanked the vines for growing so fast.

The vines grew longer and longer.

Positive words of love and kindness seemed to help the vines grow.

I was happy that the vines listened to my positive words.

WORDS ARE IMPORTANT!

Let's practice some positive words to help us grow like the sweet potato vines.

I feel great!!

How do I show that I am feeling great?

I smile.

I say nice things to myself and to others.

What are some other ways to show that you're feeling great?

I am happy to be me.

I can feel great even if someone is not great to me.

I can feel great even if the weather is bad.

I can change how I feel even if I am feeling sad.

I am thankful

- I am thankful for my home
- I am thankful for my friends
- I am thankful for my family
- I am thankful for my sweet potato vines

THANK YOU!

What else are you thankful for?

Today I remembered to thank my friends for playing with me.

I'm thankful for my bed
I'm thankful for my sled
I'm thankful for the night
I'm thankful for my sight

Thank you for my amazing life

Today I am choosing

LOVE

I **love** my mom

I **love** my dad

I **love** me

I **love** my home

I **love** my shoes

I **love** my bed

I **love** trees

Today I reminded myself to love me.

I love my hair.

I love my eyes.

I love my clothes. I love my toes. I love my ears.

I love my nose.

It's easy to love

When I'm feeling great

I must remember to love

If I'm feeling hate

I wish for

I wish to be happy and healthy like the sweet potato vines.

As you play or go for a walk, what happy things do you wish for?

What do you love to do?

What games do you like to play?

What musical instruments do you like?

Where do you love to go?

The sweet potato vines loved to grow all over the yard.

Draw or find pictures of places to go.

I remember the story of the sweet potato vines. The more positive words they heard, the faster they grew and the healthier they looked.

I must talk to myself in the same way.

I am a wonderful person.

I am always thinking good thoughts about myself and others.

I am happy.

I want to feel good, so I think good thoughts.

I like me.

I say positive words to myself like I did to the sweet potato vines.

Happy

Love

Laughter

Fun

What other positive words can you think of?

I hope you grow like the sweet potato vines, healthy and amazing.

Always have a sunny smile and happy thoughts.

About the Author

Maltee McMahon is an instructor/trainer and motivational speaker. She has a Bachelor's and Master's degree in Business Administration/Management. She is also a certified facilitator for True Colors® Personality Assessment and an instructor trainer for Certified Infant Massage.

A former Dale Carnegie instructor, McMahon has worked with all ages and levels of management to motivate and inspire.

Ingram Content Group UK Ltd.
Milton Keynes UK
UKHW050810280623
424180UK00007B/40